P9-DNM-526

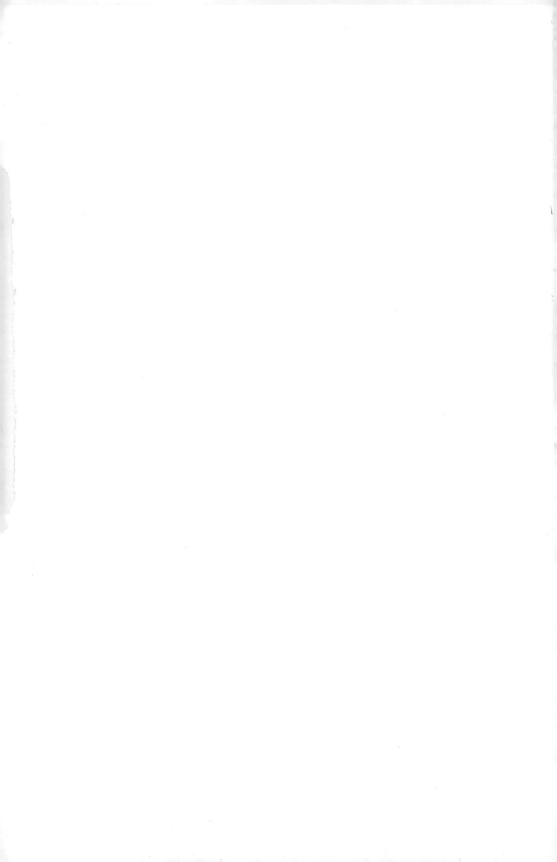

Dear Parent:
Your child's love of reading starts here!

Every child learns to read in a different way and at his or her own speed. Some go back and forth between reading levels and read favorite books again and again. Others read through each level in order. You can help your young reader improve and become more confident by encouraging his or her own interests and abilities. From books your child reads with you to the first books he or she reads alone, there are I Can Read Books for every stage of reading:

SHARED READING
Basic language, word repetition, and whimsical illustrations, ideal for sharing with your emergent reader

BEGINNING READING
Short sentences, familiar words, and simple concepts for children eager to read on their own

READING WITH HELP
Engaging stories, longer sentences, and language play for developing readers

READING ALONE
Complex plots, challenging vocabulary, and high-interest topics for the independent reader

I Can Read Books have introduced children to the joy of reading since 1957. Featuring award-winning authors and illustrators and a fabulous cast of beloved characters, I Can Read Books set the standard for beginning readers.

A lifetime of discovery begins with the magical words **"I Can Read!"**

Visit www.icanread.com for information on enriching your child's reading experience.

Visit www.zonderkidz.com/icanread for more faith-based I Can Read! titles from Zonderkidz.

HOORAY!

_____

can read this book!

ZONDERkidz

My First SHARED READING

I Can Read!

The Beginner's Bible

Read Through the Bible

God Makes the World

Noah and the Great Big Ark

David and the Giant

Queen Esther Saves Her People

Daniel and the Lions' Den

Jonah and the Giant Fish

Jesus Is Born

Jesus Saves the World

8 Bible Stories for Beginning Readers

ZONDERKIDZ

The Beginner's Bible Read Through the Bible
Copyright © 2007 by Zondervan
Illustrations © 2017 by Zondervan

An **I Can Read Book**

Requests for information should be addressed to:

Zonderkidz, 3900 *Sparks Drive SE, Grand Rapids, Michigan 49546*

ISBN 978-0-310-75280-6 (hardcover)

Titles include:
- *The Beginner's Bible God Makes the World* ISBN: 9780310764649
- *The Beginner's Bible Noah and the Great Big Ark* ISBN: 9780310760290
- *The Beginner's Bible David and the Giant* ISBN: 9780310760481
- *The Beginner's Bible Queen Esther Saves Her People* ISBN: 9780310764786
- *The Beginner's Bible Daniel and the Lions' Den* ISBN: 9780310760412
- *The Beginner's Bible Jonah and the Giant Fish* ISBN: 9780310760443
- *The Beginner's Bible Jesus Is Born* ISBN: 9780310760504
- *The Beginner's Bible Jesus Saves the World* ISBN: 9780310760368

All Scripture quotations, unless otherwise indicated are taken from the Holy Bible, *New International Reader's Version®, NIrV®.* Copyright © 1995, 1996, 1998, 2014 by Biblica, Inc.® Used by permission of Zondervan. All rights reserved worldwide. www. zondervan.com. The "NIrV" and "New International Reader's Version" are trademarks registered in the United States Patent and Trademark Office by Biblica, Inc.®

Any internet addresses (websites, blogs, etc.) and telephone numbers in this book are offered as a resource. They are not intended in any way to be or imply an endorsement by Zondervan, nor does Zondervan vouch for the content of these sites and numbers for the life of this book.

No part of this publication may be reproduced, stored in a retrieval system, or transmitted in any form or by any means—electronic, mechanical, photocopy, recording, or any other—except for brief quotations in printed reviews, without the prior permission of the publisher.

Zonderkidz is a trademark of Zondervan.

I Can Read® and I Can Read Book® are trademarks of HarperCollins Publishers.

Illustrator: Denis Alonso
Art Direction: Diane Mielke

Printed in Korea

22 23 24 25 26 27 28 /SAM/ 15 14 13 12 11 10 9 8 7 6 5 4 3 2 1

Table of Contents

God saw everything he had made.
And it was very good.
–*Genesis 1:31*

God Makes the World

In the beginning,
the world was empty.
But God had a plan.

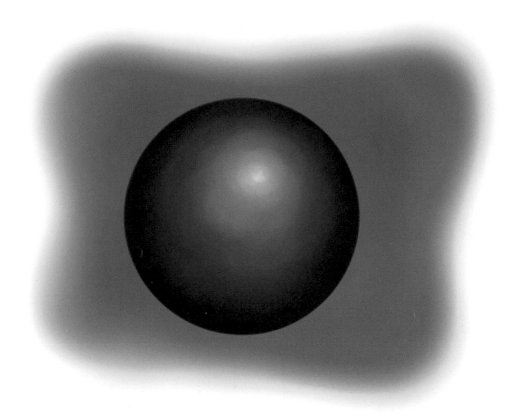

"I will make
many good things,"
God said.

On day one God said,
"I will make day and night."
So he did.

On day two God split
the water from the air.
He said, "Here are the sky
and sea."

God made land on day three.
Plants grew on the land.
Fruit trees grew there too.

On day four God put the sun
and the moon in the sky.

On day five
God made birds
to fly in the sky.

He made fish to swim
in the ocean.

Day six was busy.
God made the rest
of the animals.

Then God made the first man.
God named him Adam.
God loved Adam.

God rested on day seven.
He was so happy!

Adam was happy too.

God put Adam in a garden.

The garden was called Eden.

Adam took care of Eden.
He took care of the animals.

He even named all the animals.
"You will be called a 'parrot.'
You will be called a 'butterfly.'"

One day God made Eve.
She helped Adam take care
of the garden and the animals.

God gave Adam and Eve one rule.
God said, "Do not eat
fruit from this tree."

Later, a sneaky snake
was in the tree.

"Eve, you can eat this fruit.
It is fine!" the snake said.

Eve ate the fruit.

Then Adam ate the fruit too.

God was sad.

They had broken his one rule.

This was called "sin."

"Eve gave me the fruit,"
Adam said.

"Snake tricked me," Eve said.

God said, "Snake,
you must move on your
belly and eat dust."

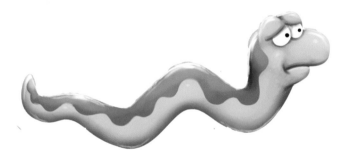

God told Adam and Eve,
"You must leave.
You did not follow my rule."

Adam and Eve left the garden.
They were very sad.

But God would always love them.
He made another plan.

One day, God would send Jesus.
Jesus would save everyone
from their sins.

(Noah) sent the dove out from the ark again. In the evening the dove returned to him. There in its beak was a freshly picked olive leaf! So Noah knew that the water on the earth had gone down.

–Genesis 8:10–11

Noah and the Great Big Ark

Genesis 6–9

ZONDERkidz
.com

A long time ago, people
were very mean to each other.
They forgot about God.

They did not love God.

This made God very sad.

But Noah was a good man.
Noah and his family
loved God.

God had a big plan.

He told Noah,

"I am going to start over."

God told Noah to build a boat.

The boat was called an ark.

And Noah did what God said.

God said, "I will save you.
I will save your family
and two of each animal."

Noah built the boat.

God sent the animals.

"Hi, cats and dogs!
Hi, bears and birds!"

There was food.

There was family.

There were God's animals.

One day, God closed the door.
Then God sent a big storm!

Rain began to fall.

It rained and rained.

The ark rocked and rocked.

The ark bumped up and down,
up and down.

Noah prayed.

Noah's family prayed.

The animals watched.

God took care of Noah.
God took care of his family.

God kept all of them safe.

The rain fell for days,
and days,
and days.

The earth was covered
with water!

"Shhhhh," Noah said.
Something was different.

It was quiet!

The rain had stopped!

The ark was still!

Noah said,
"Dove, please find land."
But Dove did not find land.

Noah said, "Dove, try again."
Dove did find land!

One day, the ark
bumped into land.
Slowly, the water
started drying up.

God said, "Time to go!"
He helped Noah open the ark.
The animals went to play.

God said, "See the rainbow?
It means I will not cover the earth
with water again.
I promise!"

"The LORD doesn't rescue by using a sword or a spear. And everyone who is here will know it. The battle belongs to the LORD."
—*1 Samuel 17:47*

David and the Giant

Goliath was a big giant.

He was mean.

He wanted to fight
King Saul's army.

The army was afraid.

They ran away from Goliath.

"We do not want to
fight you!" they cried.

David took care of sheep.

He loved God.

David's brothers were in
the king's army.

One day, David took food
to his brothers.
He heard about the giant.

David said, "The giant
does not scare me!"

"Let me fight the giant,"
David said to the king.
"God will help me."

"The giant is big,"
King Saul said.
"And you are too young."

"Please, let me fight him,"
said David.

So the king gave David
armor to wear.

David said,

"I do not need armor."

He was not used to wearing it.

David picked up some stones.
He was getting ready
to fight the giant.

David saw the giant.

The giant saw David.

"You are too small.
I will beat you!" said
Goliath.

"You will not beat me,"
said David.
"God will help me!"

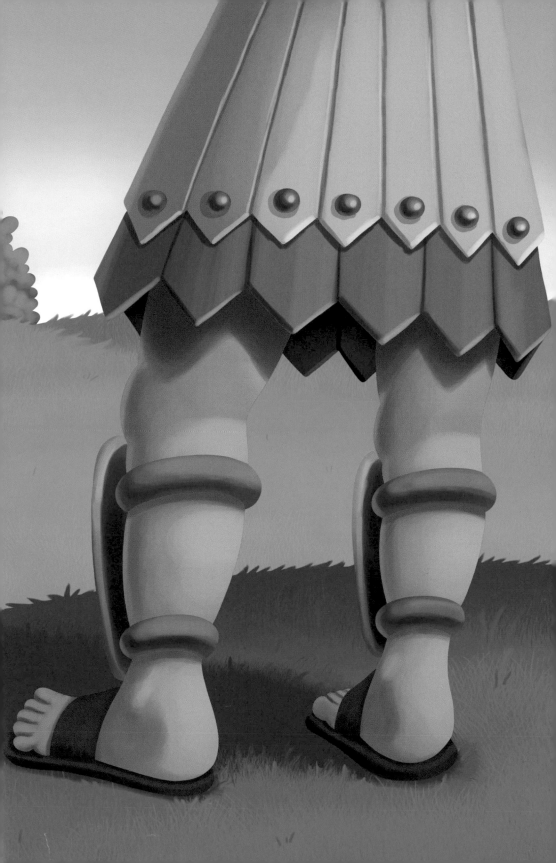

David took a stone.
He threw it at Goliath.

The stone hit Goliath
on the head.

Goliath fell down.
David won!

The men in Goliath's army
were scared.

They ran away.

The men in King Saul's army
were happy.

David was a hero.

"God is great!" yelled David.
"He helped me!"

"Who knows? It's possible that you became queen for a time just like this."

—*Esther 4:14*

Queen Esther Saves
Her People

ZONDERkidz
.com

Once there was a king
who needed a new queen.

"Let us find you
a new queen,"
said the king's men.

Esther and Mordecai
were cousins.
They lived in the king's land.

They loved God.

Mordecai said,

"You could be the new queen."

So Esther got ready.

And she went to see the king.

The king liked Esther.

He said, "Will you be my queen?"

Esther said, "Yes."

The king had a helper.

His name was Haman.

He was a mean man.

Esther and her cousin were Jewish.

Haman hated Jewish people.

He did not love God.

Haman had a plan.

He went to the king.

"Jewish people are bad.
Help me get rid of them."

The king did not know
Queen Esther was Jewish.
The king was tricked!

God's people were in danger!
Mordecai heard about the plan.

Mordecai went to tell Esther.

"Esther! Save God's people.
Maybe that is why
God made you the queen!"

Esther needed a plan.

It would not be easy.

But Esther was brave.

She would help God's people.

Esther made a nice dinner.

She invited the king and Haman.

The king and Haman were happy.
The king asked, "What can I do
for you, Esther?"

"Haman tricked you!
You signed a law," Esther said.

"It says to get rid of all Jews.
I am Jewish!"

The king was mad!

He did not like to be tricked.

The king said, "Get Haman!
Arrest him now!"

The king made Mordecai
his new helper.

The king was happy with Mordecai.

The king was happy with Esther.

The Jewish people were saved!

Esther was a hero.

God used Esther
to save his people.

"My God sent his angel. And his angel shut the mouths of the lions. They haven't hurt me at all."
—*Daniel 6:22*

ZONDERkidz™

SHARED READING

My First

I Can Read!

The Beginner's Bible®

Daniel and the Lions' Den

Daniel was a good man.

He loved God very much.

The king loved Daniel.

Daniel helped the king.

Because he loved God, some
men did not like Daniel.
The men made an evil plan.

The men went to the king.

"King, you are a great man,"
they said.

"People should pray
only to you."

The men said, "If they do not,
we will put them
in the lions' den."

The men wanted to get Daniel
in big trouble.

The king said, "Okay."
He did not know it was
a trap for Daniel.

Daniel prayed only to God.

The men saw Daniel praying.
He did not stop praying to God.

The men told the king
about Daniel.

"King, your helper Daniel does not obey your rule," the men said.

"Daniel was praying
to God. Not to you."

The men had tricked the king.

Guards came to take
Daniel away to the
lions' den.

The king shook his head.
The rule said pray
only to the king.

But Daniel would not stop.

He would pray only to God.

The king did not
want to hurt Daniel.

The king said, "Daniel, I hope your God will save you."

Daniel was thrown into
the lions' den.
The king was very sad.

Daniel prayed to God.
He asked God to watch
over him.

So God sent his angel
to help Daniel.
Daniel was safe all night.

In the morning,
the king woke up.
He ran to see Daniel.

The king called, "Daniel,
are you okay?
Did your God save you?"

"Yes," said Daniel.
"God's angel helped me
with the lions!"

The king was so happy!
"Come with me, Daniel."

The king told all his people,
"Daniel's God is great!
Let us pray only to God."

The LORD gave the fish a command.
And it spit Jonah up onto dry land.

—*Jonah 2:10*

ZONDER**kidz**™ My First SHARED READING **I Can Read!**

The Beginner's Bible®

Jonah and the Giant Fish

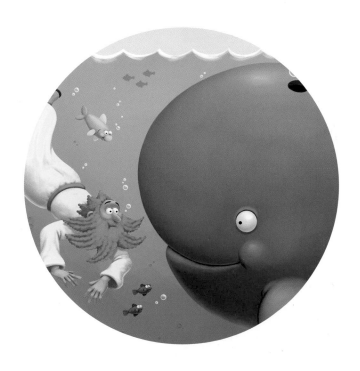

Z **ZONDERkidz**™
.com

Jonah told people about God.

One day, God told Jonah
to go on a trip.

God said, "People in Nineveh
are doing bad things.
Please go there and talk
to them."

Jonah was not happy.

He did not want to go.

So he ran away!

Jonah talked to some men.
"Please let me sail away
with you."

The boat went out to sea.

It went right into a storm!

The wind blew and blew.

The waves went up and down,
up and down.

The men were scared.

"Where is Jonah?" they called.

Jonah was taking a nap.

"Get up, Jonah," they said.
"We are in big trouble!
Say a prayer for us!"

"God is upset.

I ran away from him!"

Jonah said.

"He wants me to go back.

He wants me to go to

Nineveh."

"How do we stop this storm?"
asked the men.

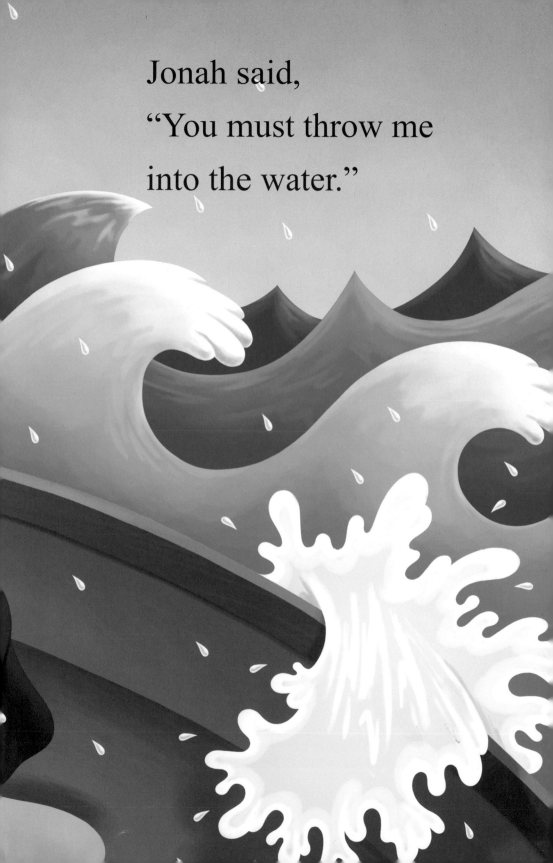

Jonah said,
"You must throw me
into the water."

The men tossed Jonah
into the water.

The storm stopped.
The sea was calm!

But up from the water
swam a big fish.

The fish swallowed Jonah.

Jonah sat in the big fish
for three days
and three nights.

"I am sorry I ran away.
Thank you, God, for
saving me," said Jonah.

Then God said, "Big fish!
Put Jonah back on dry land!"

God said, "Jonah, go to Nineveh.
Tell the people to stop
doing bad things."

This time Jonah was brave.

He knew God was with him.

Jonah went to talk
to the people of Nineveh.

Jonah told the people,
"Stop doing bad things!"

They listened to Jonah.

God forgave Jonah.

God forgave the people.

He loves all his people.

There were shepherds living out in the fields nearby.
It was night, and they were taking care of their sheep.
An angel of the Lord appeared to them. And the glory of
the Lord shone around them. They were terrified. But the
angel said to them, "Do not be afraid. I bring you good
news. It will bring great joy for all the people. Today in the
town of David a Savior has been born to you.
He is the Messiah, the Lord."
—*Luke 2:8–11*

Jesus Is Born

There was a girl named Mary.
She loved God very much.

Mary knew a man called Joseph.
They were going to
be married soon.

One day, God sent an
angel to Mary.

The angel said,
"You will have a baby boy.
He is God's Son."

Mary asked, "How can it be?
I am not married yet."

The angel said to Mary,
"God can do anything!"

Joseph and Mary got married.
They loved God's Son
growing in Mary's tummy.

Joseph and Mary had to go
on a long trip.
They went to Bethlehem.
It was far away.

Mary and Joseph needed
a place to stay.
Mary was going to have
the baby soon!

But there were no rooms left.
A man said, "You can sleep in
my stable."

That night, a baby boy
was born.
The baby was Jesus!

Mary wrapped Jesus in cloths.
She put him in a manger.

Angels came to some shepherds.

An angel said, "Good news!

A Savior was born today!"

The shepherds went to see
Baby Jesus.

The shepherds were so happy.
They shouted, "Jesus is born!
He is our Savior!"

Some time later,
wise men saw a new star.
It meant a baby king
was born.

The wise men followed the star.
On their way, they stopped
to see King Herod.

The wise men wanted
to ask King Herod
about the baby king.

King Herod was mean.

He tried to trick the wise men.

"Find the baby king for me
so I can worship him," he said.

King Herod had a plan.
He wanted to get rid
of Jesus.

The star led the wise men
all the way to Jesus.
They gave Jesus gifts.

The angel told the wise men,
"Do not go back
to King Herod."
So the wise men took
a different road home.

When King Herod found out,
he was very angry.

King Herod yelled,
"Find the boy!
I am the only king!"

Then an angel told Joseph,
"Take your family far away.
You are not safe here."

So Joseph took Mary and
Jesus far, far away.

Jesus grew and grew.
Mary and Joseph loved
Jesus so much.

One day, an angel
said to Joseph,
"It is safe.
Now you can go home."

Joseph, Mary, and Jesus
went back home.
Jesus grew up and told
many people about God's love.

"I am the way and the truth and the life.
No one comes to the Father except through me."
—*John 14:6*

ZONDER**kidz** My First / SHARED READING / **I Can Read!**

The Beginner's Bible

Jesus Saves the World

ZONDER**kidz**
.com

The day Jesus was born
was a very special day.

Angels came to tell the
good news!

People were so happy
Jesus was born.

Jesus was born to save us
from our sins.

Jesus grew up.

He was a good boy.

He helped his mother, Mary.

He helped his father, Joseph.

Jesus helped other people too.

When he was grown,
his cousin John
baptized him.

Then Jesus went to work.

He told people all about God.

Jesus told his friends
about God too.

Jesus' friends helped tell
others about God's love.

Jesus told the people
to love each other.

Jesus also did things
called miracles.

One day, Jesus and his friends
were in a boat.
It started to storm.

His friends were scared.

"Jesus, can you help?" they cried.

Jesus said, "Stop, Storm."

The storm stopped.
It was a miracle!

Jesus also healed people.
He helped a sick little
girl get better.
Another miracle!

Jesus healed blind people.

"I can see!" the man said.

Jesus loved all children.
Even when he was very busy,
he stopped to talk to them.

But not all people loved Jesus.
Some made a plan to stop him.

Jesus went to a garden.

He prayed,

"I will do what you want, God."

"I am ready to give my life
to save people
from their sins," he said.

The bad men took Jesus away.

They nailed Jesus to a
big cross made of wood.
He died on the cross.

Everyone who loved Jesus
was very sad.

They put his body in a tomb.

Soldiers watched over it.

Jesus' friends went to the tomb.

An angel said to them,

"Jesus is not here.

He is risen!"

Soon, Jesus went to
see his friends.
They were so happy!

Then it was time for Jesus
to go to heaven.
But he will come back one day!

More Zonderkidz I CAN READ! books for you to love:

9780310715849

9780310715856

9780310715863

9780310715870

9780310716044

9780310716051

9780310716068

9780310716075

9780310720997

9780310725015

9780310760092

9780310760245

9780310726791

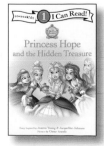

9780310732501

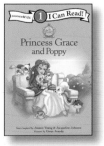

9780310726777

9780310732518

Building foundations of faith with children for over 30 years!

9780310750130
$18.99 / Hardcover

The Beginner's Bible® has been a favorite with young children and their parents since its release in 1989 with over 25 million products sold. While several updates have been made since its early days, *The Beginner's Bible*® will continue to build a foundation of faith in little ones for many more years to come.

Full of faith and fun, *The Beginner's Bible*® is a wonderful gift for any child. The easy-to-read text and bright, full-color illustrations on every page make it a perfect way to introduce young children to the stories and characters of the Bible. With new vibrant three-dimensional art and compelling text, more than 90 Bible stories come to life. Kids ages 6 and under will enjoy the fun illustrations of Noah helping the elephant onto the ark, Jonah praying inside the fish, and more, as they discover *The Beginner's Bible*® just like millions of children before. *The Beginner's Bible*® was named the 2006 Retailers Choice Award winner in Children's Nonfiction.

More products from *The Beginner's Bible*® to discover:

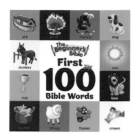

The Beginner's Bible
First 100 Bible Words
9780310766858

The Beginner's Bible
Learn Your Letters
9780310770244

The Beginner's Bible
All Aboard Noah's Ark
9780310768678

The Beginner's Bible
Little Lamb's Christmas
9780310770589

The Beginner's Bible Super
Girls of the Bible Sticker
and Activity Book
9780310751182

The Beginner's Bible
All About Jesus Sticker
and Activity Book
9780310746935

The Beginner's Bible
People of the Bible
9780310765035